HART·BEAT

The illustration on page 42 is from the
Lindisfarne Gospels (MS Cotton Nero D.
iv, f 139), reproduced by courtesy of the
British Library.

Published by BBC Books,
a division of BBC Enterprises Limited,
Woodlands, 80 Wood Lane,
London W12 0TT
First published 1988

ISBN 0 563 20652 7

Set in 9/10 Univers by Redwood Burn,
Trowbridge, Wilts.
Printed and bound in Great Britain by
Redwood Burn Limited,
Trowbridge, Wilts.
Colour separations by Technik,
Berkhamsted, Herts.
Cover printed by Belmont Press,
Northampton

HART·BEAT

TONY HART

MARGOT WILSON

&

JOANNA KIRK

Compiled by · CHRISTOPHER PILKINGTON
with Jane Harrison
Photographs · BARRY BOXALL
Design · EVE WHITE

BBC BOOKS

INTRODUCTION

The Hartbeat Book is full of all sorts of picture-making ideas for all ages. It includes popular items from the television series and new ideas. We get so many letters asking us to explain again things we have shown on *Hartbeat*, so here is a chance for you to follow a step-by-step guide to the most popular pictures.

Our materials are always easily obtainable, and our ideas come from the things we see around us and the materials we have at hand.

The book is divided up into ten exciting themes which Margot, Joanna and myself have enjoyed working on. We have also selected some of your Gallery pictures. The range and standard of your pictures is tremendous. We enjoy looking through them all.

One of the nice things you say to us is that you often use our ideas, but sometimes make changes, perhaps by choosing different materials. That is terrific, it shows you are interested in making things work for you.

There is great satisfaction to be had by making a picture of your own. We hope that this book will help you to really enjoy the art of making pictures.

TONY HART

Born in Maidstone in 1925.

Tony studied Graphics at Maidstone College of Art.

His first job with the BBC was in 1952.

In 1964, *Vision On* established Tony as part of a team presenting visual ideas on Children's Television.

Take Hart (1977) was a series concentrating on Tony's unique gifts in presenting and encouraging young artists.

Hartbeat (1985) further developed Tony's style of presentation and broadened the range of work and materials. It also brought together Tony, Margot Wilson and Joanna Kirk.

Outside his television work, Tony works as a freelance artist and has contributed cartoons and graphics to organisations ranging from International Computers to Cambridge University. He lectures and holds demonstrations and workshops. He has written many books on art, ranging from design, lettering to how children develop their skills in Art.

M A R G O T   W I L S O N

Born in Ealing in 1962.

She began her career in art and design in 1980, with a one-year foundation course.

During her first year, she decided which area to specialise in. This led to a B.A. degree course in Graphic Design.

Margot stayed at St Martins for a three-year degree course from 1981 to 1984.

During her third year at St Martins, she was offered the chance to appear with Tony Hart on *Hartbeat.*

Since leaving college, Margot has combined appearing on *Hartbeat* with working as magazine designer for The

Observer, Elle, Tatler and *The Sunday Times* magazine.

Margot has a notebook which she fills with ideas from magazines, cuttings etc. 'Must be observant. From my collected materials ideas can be worked out. I am particularly interested in how objects are constructed. I generally use coloured card and paper, if you don't want to buy card you can collect old boxes and paint them.'

'My ideas can take time to put together, but if you think each stage through and persevere they are great fun to make and very satisfying and worth keeping.'

Margot Wilson

J O A N N A   K I R K

Born in 1963.

In 1980 Joanna did a one-year foundation course at West Surrey College of Art and Design.

She went on to do a three-year degree, from 1981 to 1984, in Fine Art at Goldsmiths College.

When she left college Joanna got a studio with other artists, and was then offered the opportunity to appear as presenter on *Hartbeat.*

'I'm showing that making things can be

really good fun – using materials from around the house and outside, you can make brilliant things with imagination. Don't be scared of having a go and making mistakes. I get lots of ideas from seeing things around me, things that everyone has access to – magazines, newspapers, books. Ideas don't just happen! Lots of artists today are doing things which are lively and imaginative, art is not just restricted to what's in galleries.' Jo's own large pastel drawings are currently being exhibited and sold.

Joanna Kirk.

CONTENTS

UNDERNEATH >>>

CONSTRUCTION

YOU WILL NEED

White paper
Pencil (*soft lead*)
Thick marker pen
Rubber (*putty rubber is best*)

2 Draw over the base shapes with thick permanent marker pen.

3 Add details to these guidelines. Rub out all pencil lines when finished. Putty rubber is best as it picks up the bits when you have finished rubbing out.

4 Adding extra 'whizz' lines above the ears helps give the impression of movement.

1 Use the basic shapes of squares, triangles and circles as the construction lines for this picture.

PLASTER TILE

1 Pour water into bucket and sprinkle handfuls of plaster of Paris into the water. The recipe is: 2 of plaster of Paris to 1 of water. When 'islands' of plaster appear on top of the water, then mix thoroughly.

2 Quickly pour mixture into silver foil tray (freezer trays are good to use). Shake the container until the plaster is level – you must move fast, as the plaster sets in minutes.

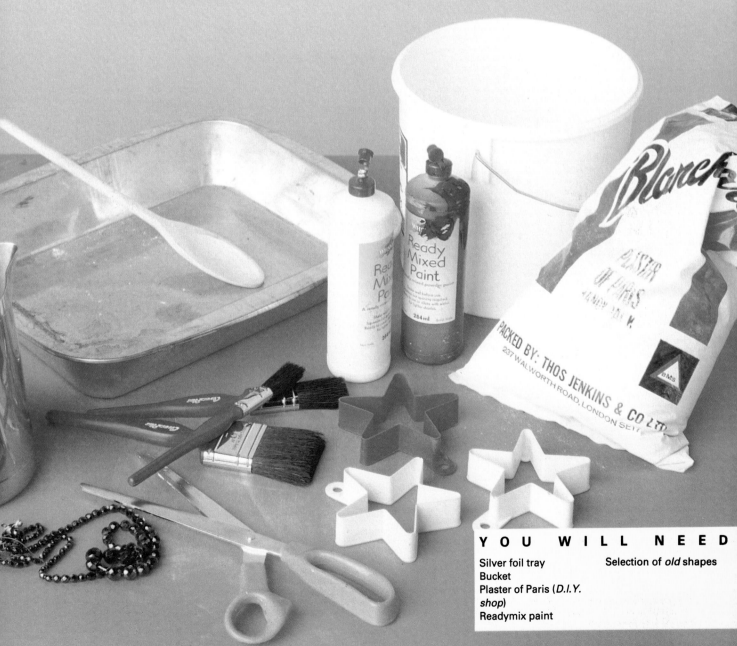

YOU WILL NEED

Silver foil tray
Bucket
Plaster of Paris (*D.I.Y. shop*)
Readymix paint

Selection of *old* shapes

3 Quickly place *old* objects into the plaster. The plaster will be fully set within five minutes.

4 Remove the objects to reveal their prints. Paint over the surface with a light colour. When dry remove the plaster from the foil to reveal the tile. You can make the surface shiny by using a clear varnish.

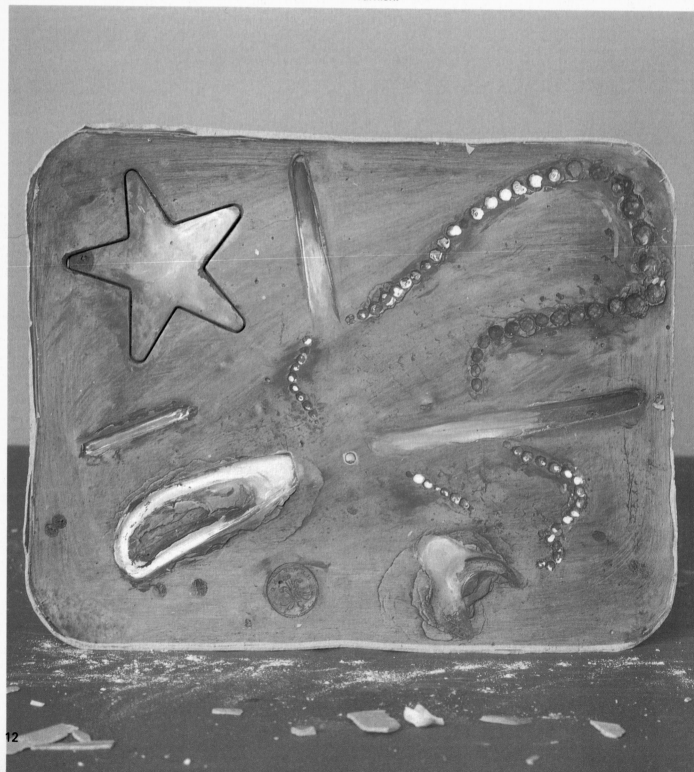

MARGOT WILSON
SKELETON

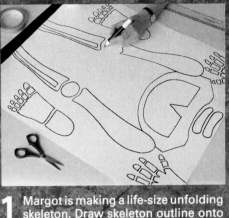

1 Margot is making a life-size unfolding skeleton. Draw skeleton outline onto white card. Make your own style of skeleton. The bones don't have to fit!

2 Cut out your bones and stick them onto the two sheets of black card. Now cut both cards into three equal sections, making a total of six equal strips.

YOU WILL NEED

2 thick black sheets of A1 card	Masking tape
2 thin white sheets of A1 card	Sticky tape
	Glue stick
Scissors	Black pen

3 Re-join the six equal strips by sticking masking tape on the back. Leave a slight gap between each section – this will allow the strips to bend and unfold.

5 Fold up the strips to reveal the 'book-shelf' – secure the headpiece to the wall.

6 Allow the skeleton to unfold! Have fun surprising your friends again and again!

4 Disguise the end section (reverse side of the feet) as a series of books on a bookshelf or whatever!

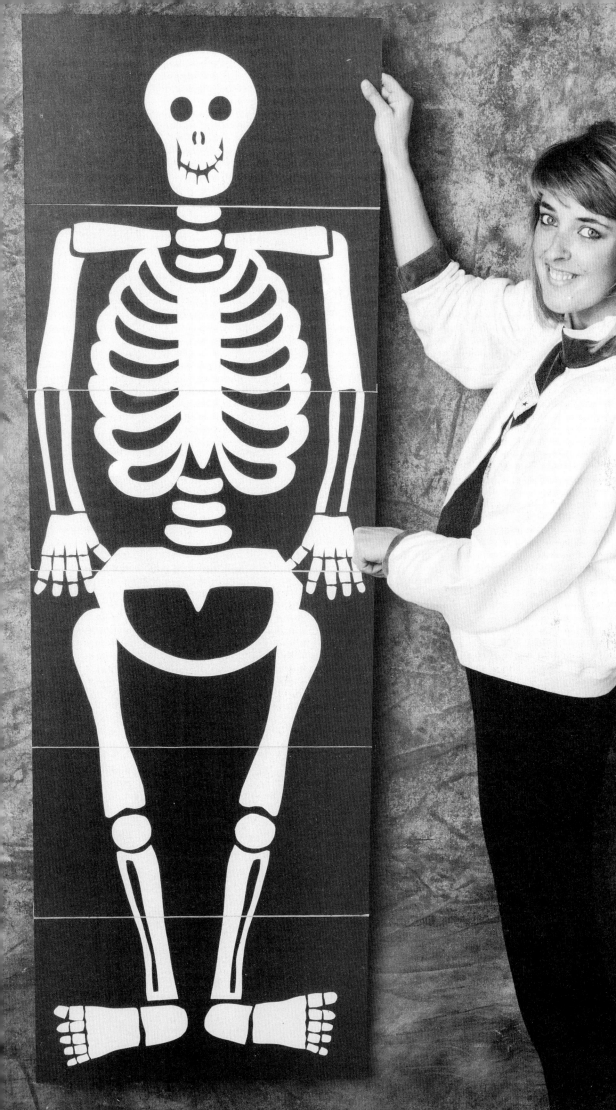

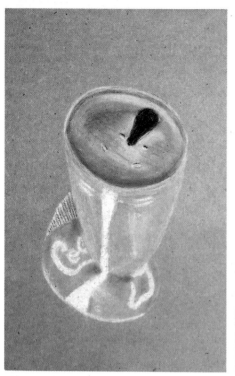

Malcolm Higgenbottom (14)

Graham Voce (7)

Becky Muirhead (11)

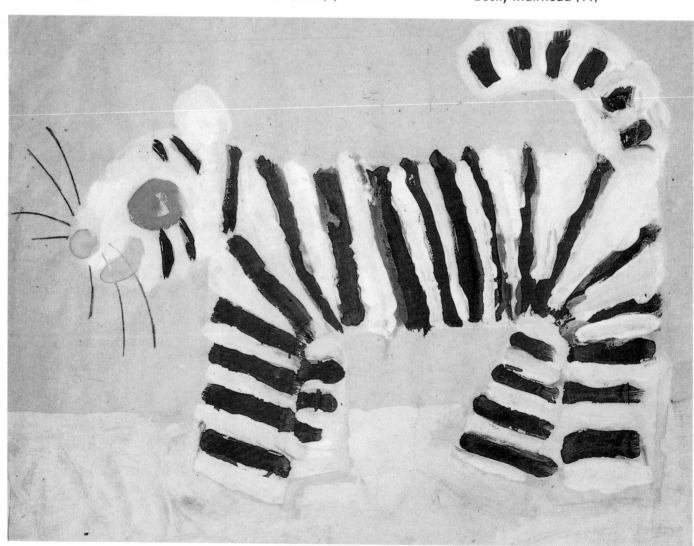

Annie Holland (5)

HANDS

CLEAN HANDPRINTS

YOU WILL NEED

Water based printing ink   Flimsy paper
(tube)
Paint roller
Washable hard board (to
roll paint on)

1 Use the roller to make a thin
film of printing ink – test roll on
old newspaper.

4 Gently peel back the
paper to reveal your
handprint. Your hands
should still be clean!

2 Place a flimsy piece of paper
onto the rolled-out ink.

3 Carefully place hand onto paper and
press down hard.

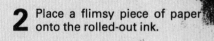

FINGERPRINT CHARACTERS

YOU WILL NEED

Water-based printing ink
Paint roller
Washable hard board
Paper
Pens

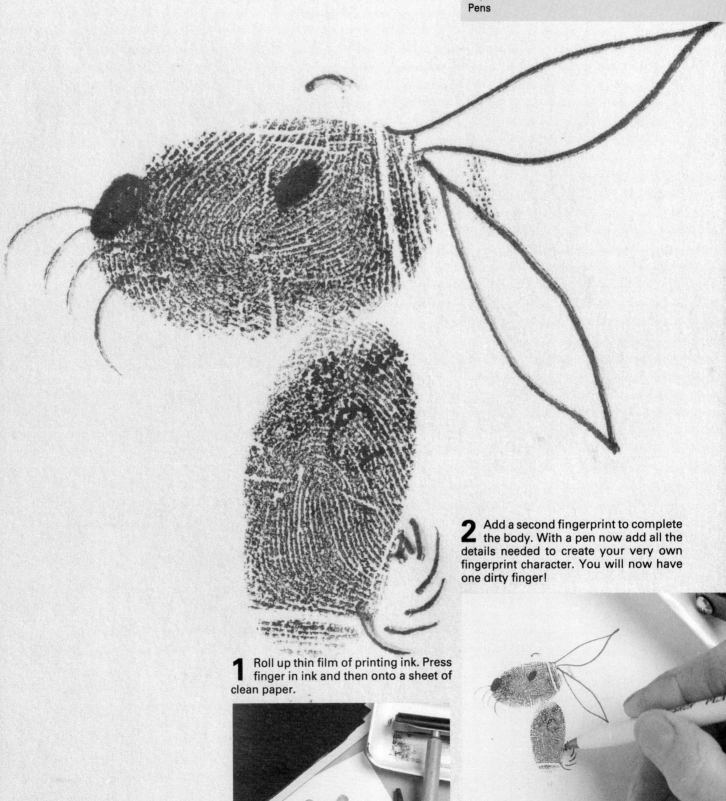

2 Add a second fingerprint to complete the body. With a pen now add all the details needed to create your very own fingerprint character. You will now have one dirty finger!

1 Roll up thin film of printing ink. Press finger in ink and then onto a sheet of clean paper.

TOY THEATRE

YOU WILL NEED

Black card	Powder paints and
White card	brushes
Thick gold card	Double-sided tape
Thin red card	Scissors
Tissue paper	Fairy tale book

1 Little Red Riding Hood
The Theatre

Theatre scenery comes in sections. There's a backdrop 520mm × 820mm painted to represent the woods. In front of this will be a series of narrow side slats 520mm × 180mm. (See picture 9 on page 22)

2 Dabbing on green paint with cotton wool creates the impression of leaves and bushes. Then add details of the trees with a brush.

3 The characters were traced from a book and stuck onto stiff card. Red Riding Hood is 280mm tall and will be mounted on a long strip of card. (40mm × 800mm)

4 Finish all characters and scenery needed. Now to make the theatre!

5 The front of the theatre is cut out from gold-coloured card. Beneath is the basic shape needed; the painted back wall, a painted floor and coloured tissue cut into sheets of black card to make the sides. Remember to cut a narrow slot at the bottom of the side pieces to allow the character 'handles' to be worked.

6 For the curtains use lightweight red card. Fold tightly into two concertina shapes. Carefully pierce a hole through the middle and thread the string.

7 Secure one edge of curtain to the back of gold card. Use paper fasteners on each side to hold the string in place.

8 This top shot shows the theatre ready for action. The black strips along the top hold all the sections together. The theatre is ready now for the show!

9 Write your own 'script' and then by moving the characters in and out, the story can be told. Draw the curtains and change the scenery when necessary!

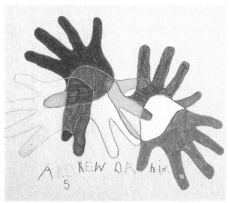

Andrew Daniels (5)

Lucy Vere (12)

Jayne Cotcher (14)

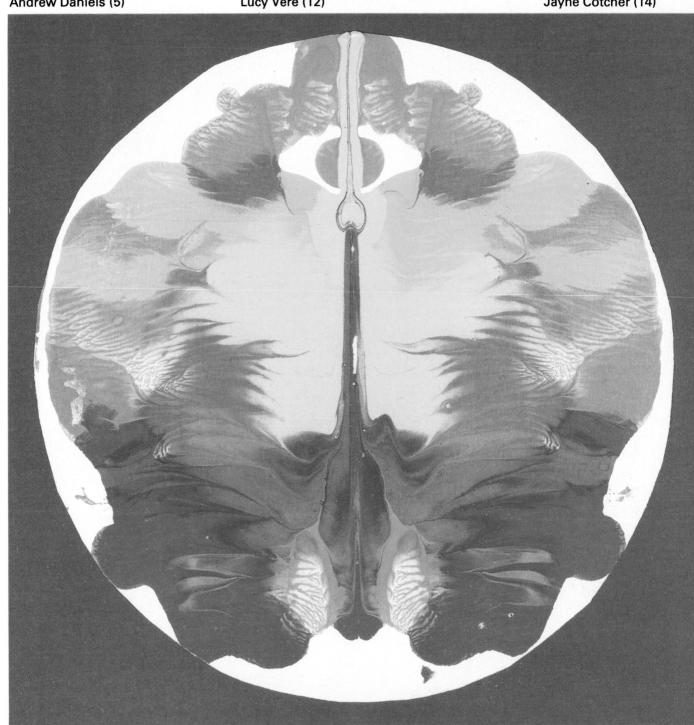

Samantha Yacomen (4)

POSITIVE/NEGATIVE

1 Use wax crayons to create 'rainbow' pattern on the greaseproof paper.

2 Place greaseproof paper over white paper. Draw directly onto the back of the greaseproof paper. It's a good idea to draw a frame round the picture.

3 Pull back to reveal the wax transfer on the white paper and a dark cat on the greaseproof side. Two for the price of one!

HE PRICE OF ONE

GALLERY

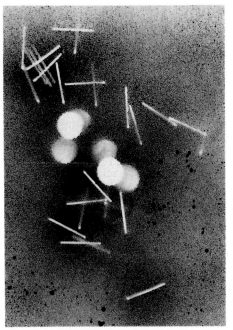

Paul Johnson (9)

Julia Bloomfield (14)

Fay Roylance (13)

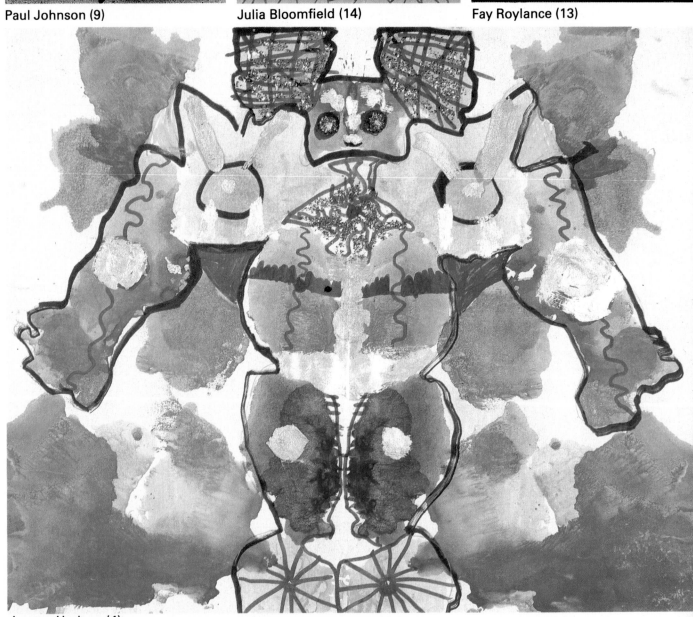

Joanna Hodson (4)

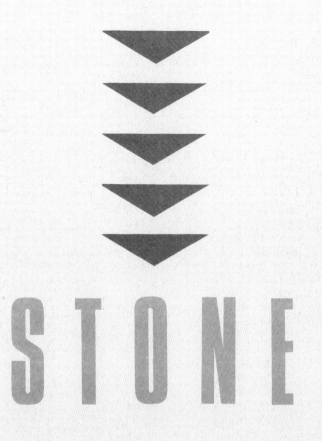

STONE

MAKE YOUR OWN ROCKS

YOU WILL NEED

Clay
Piece of stone
Boot polish (light tan colour)
Ocre yellow ink

Paintbrush
Cloth to polish finished

2 Make the clay shape you want and press it against real stone. Peel off the clay to reveal the textured surface. Allow to dry hard.

3 Colour the clay using watercolour ink; diluted yellow ocre is a good 'stone' colour.

1 How to turn clay into blocks of stone!

4 Finally, apply light tan boot polish into the clay and rub it to give that shiny, weathered-stone look.

5 Create your own Stone-Age Man: re-arrange these blocks and you've even got 'Clay-henge'!

MARGOT WILSON

BOWLING ALLEY

1 Margot makes her own box shapes, but you could use two long box lids for this exciting item.

The alley is 770mm long × 200 mm wide × 40mm high.

The skittle base is 680mm × 120mm × 35mm.

The back wall is the skittle trap and can be used to write, stencil and decorate the 'Superbowling' sign.

2 This back wall is 140mm high × 200mm wide with two side flaps 280mm long. Behind this wall can be stuck the 'Superbowling' sign. Give the alley your own name.

SUPERBOWLING!

YOU WILL NEED

2 colours of thick card	Pen/Pencil
2 colours of thin card	Ruler
Marbles	Stencil for lettering
Double-sided tape/adhesive stick	Scissors

31

3 Carefully stick the skittle base onto the alley floor. Double-sided tape is useful for this job. Make sure there's equal room around this base to allow the marbles to roll back.

4 The skittles are 80mm high and are made by folding thin card into 4 × 20mm widths (allow a flap at one end). You can decorate the skittles to your own design.

SUPERBOWLING

5 And the game is on. Roll the marbles and see how many skittles you knock over. Challenge your friends to see who can knock down all the skittles in the least number of goes. In the studio Margot's best score was three marbles to knock down the eight skittles. Beat that!

SUPERBOWLING!

Tony Hart's 'Stonehenge'

Susan Tinrue (10½)

Adrian Gallagher (9)

34

STRING &TAPE

T O N Y   H A R T
STRING CAT

YOU WILL NEED

Self-adhesive plastic
(*Get it in D.I.Y. shops –
called Fablon or
Transpaseal*)
Cord/String

Cardboard
Latex adhesive (*glue*)

1 Spread glue over non-sticky side of self-adhesive sheet. Place onto card base. Remove top protective paper to reveal the 'tacky' surface. Ready to start.

2 The cord will stick onto the surface, so carefully hold and unfold the cord to make your design. If the cord goes into the wrong place, simply pull it off and start again!

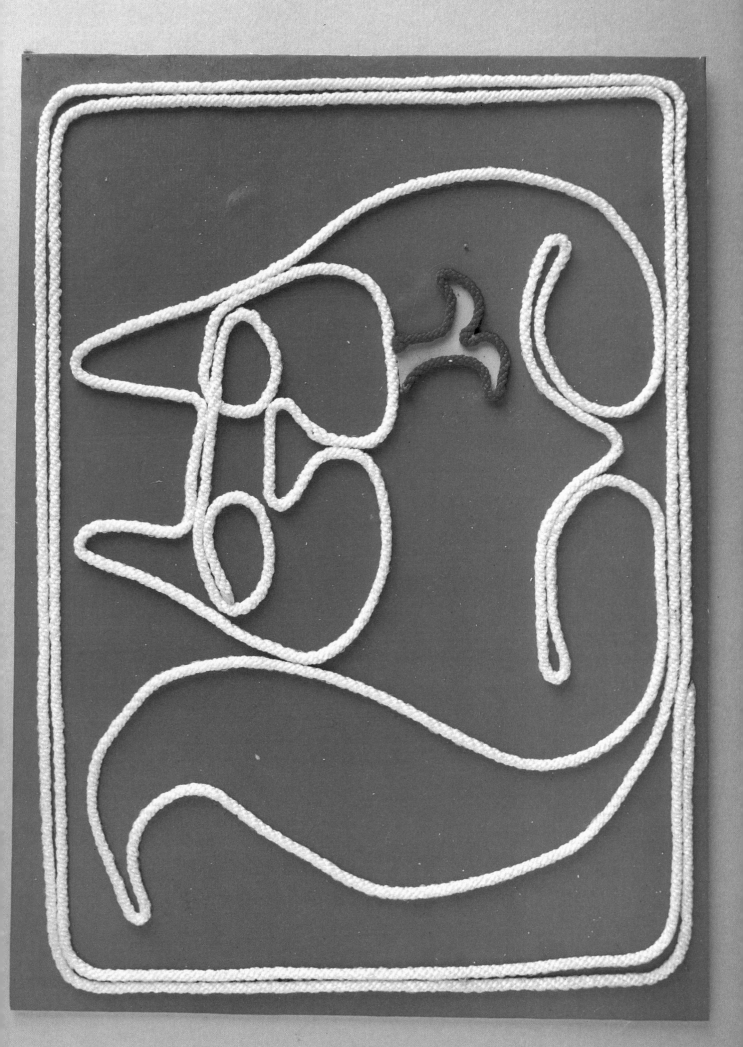

DIY VIDEO

YOU WILL NEED

Tissue/shoe box   Thick and thin card
2 till rolls (*From*   Pens
stationery shops)
Small box
Glue

1 This is an exciting way of making your own moving-picture show.

2 Draw your video-story on a till roll. Make two hollow posts, stick them into the till roll's centre and cut slots in the top.

3 In the base of the box stick two strong card posts to keep the till rolls in place. Cut two holes in the box lid to allow the posts to stick through. Cut rectangle shape out of the box side; this will be the 'screen'.

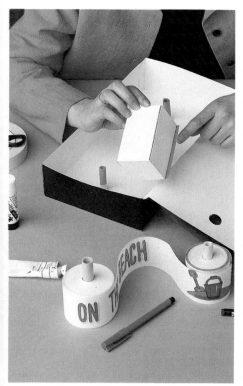

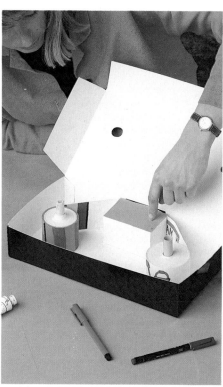

4 A small box with slight overlap on the top will help to keep the picture roll in place.

5 Thread the picture roll in front of the screen, then stick the box into position using double-sided tape.

6 Two thick strips of card fit into the slots on the till roll posts. Turn the strips to pull the picture along. The moving-picture show is now ready for viewing.

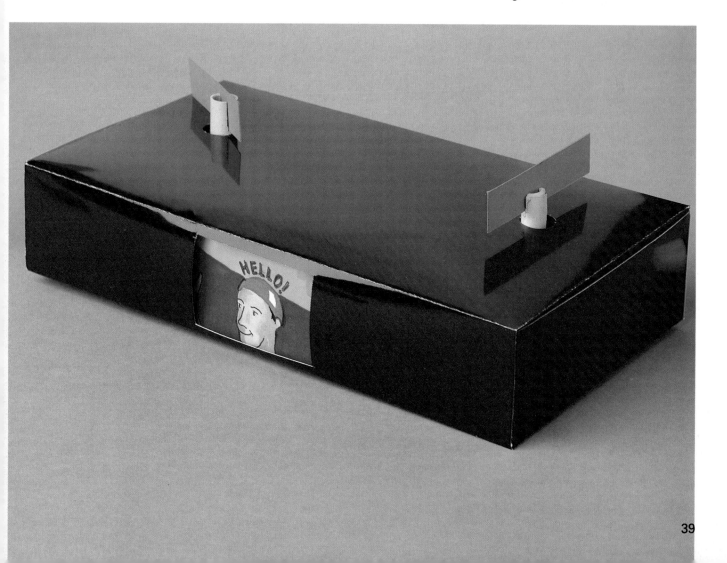

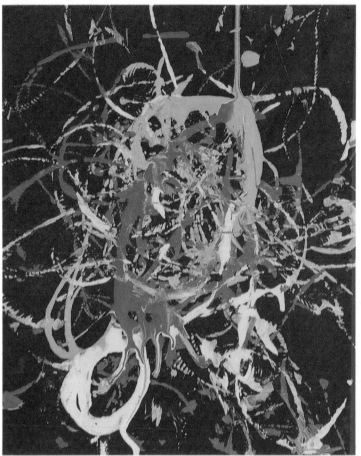

Kerry Sear (4)

Natasha Chapman (5)

Terry Mitchell (9)

CHARACTERS

CALLIGRAPHY

Calligraphy is the art of lettering. Making designs with letters can be great fun. We can buy all sorts of lettering pens and nib shapes now which make thick and thin lines, but in the Middle Ages, monks had to cut the end off feathers to make their 'quills'. These monks used coloured dyes and hours of hard work to produce stunning lettering.

There are felt tip pens and special lettering pens you can buy with a wide range of nib shapes. Coloured inks can also be bought from art and large stationery shops.

42

1 Design your letter shape with patterns on tracing paper. Trace it onto white paper. Cut out the initial letter and stick down onto black paper. Put white chalk on the back of the original design, place over the cut-out letter and trace through the internal patterns using a soft-lead pencil.

YOU WILL NEED

White chalk
Pencils
Tracing paper
Coloured pens
Metallic pen

White and black paper

2 Using coloured pens, design the colour scheme, and fill in the shapes. The more colours the more impressive it will look.

3 The gold metallic pen gives a terrific border to the design. Now take time to decorate the curly pattern within the letter. (Be grateful you don't have to keep sharpening your feather quill!!)

MARGOT WILSON
3D LETTERS

YOU WILL NEED

Thin card
Scissors
Masking tape
Ruler
Pencil

1 Here's a great way to make your name stand out! Draw and cut out your letters, or trace the big capitals from newspapers and magazines.

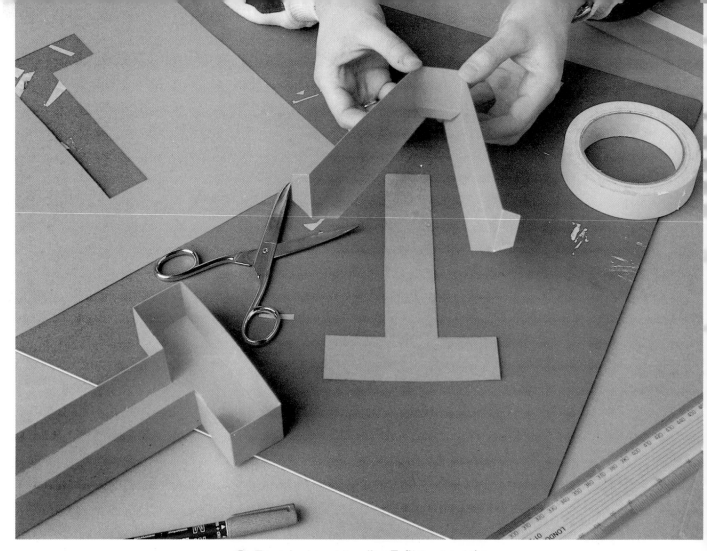

2 To make an outstanding T, first cut out the flat letter. To make the stem, measure round the flat letter, add spare length for flaps, then score, fold and stick onto the T.

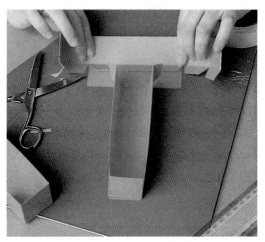

3 The top of the flat letter is made in the same way. Measure round, allow for the flaps and stick onto the top of the T. Use double-sided tape or glue to join the top with the stem.

4 The hollow T is now complete. The fiddly bit is over! Margot makes it all look very easy, but with care and by following her stages, it is all possible!

5 The hollow T needs to be mounted on card now. Place the 3-D letter over the cut-out T in the base card and secure it in place using masking tape.

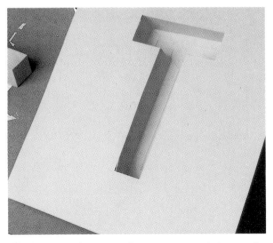

6 Turn the base card over to reveal the sunken T. All letters can be made in the same way. The more curves in the letters the more snips and folds needed.

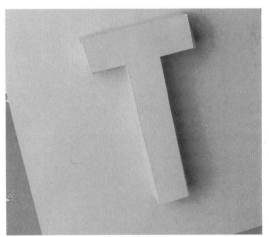

7 To make the T stand out from the base card, simply lay the base card with original T cut from it on top of the hollow T. Stick the card to the letter and then turn it over to reveal an outstanding letter!

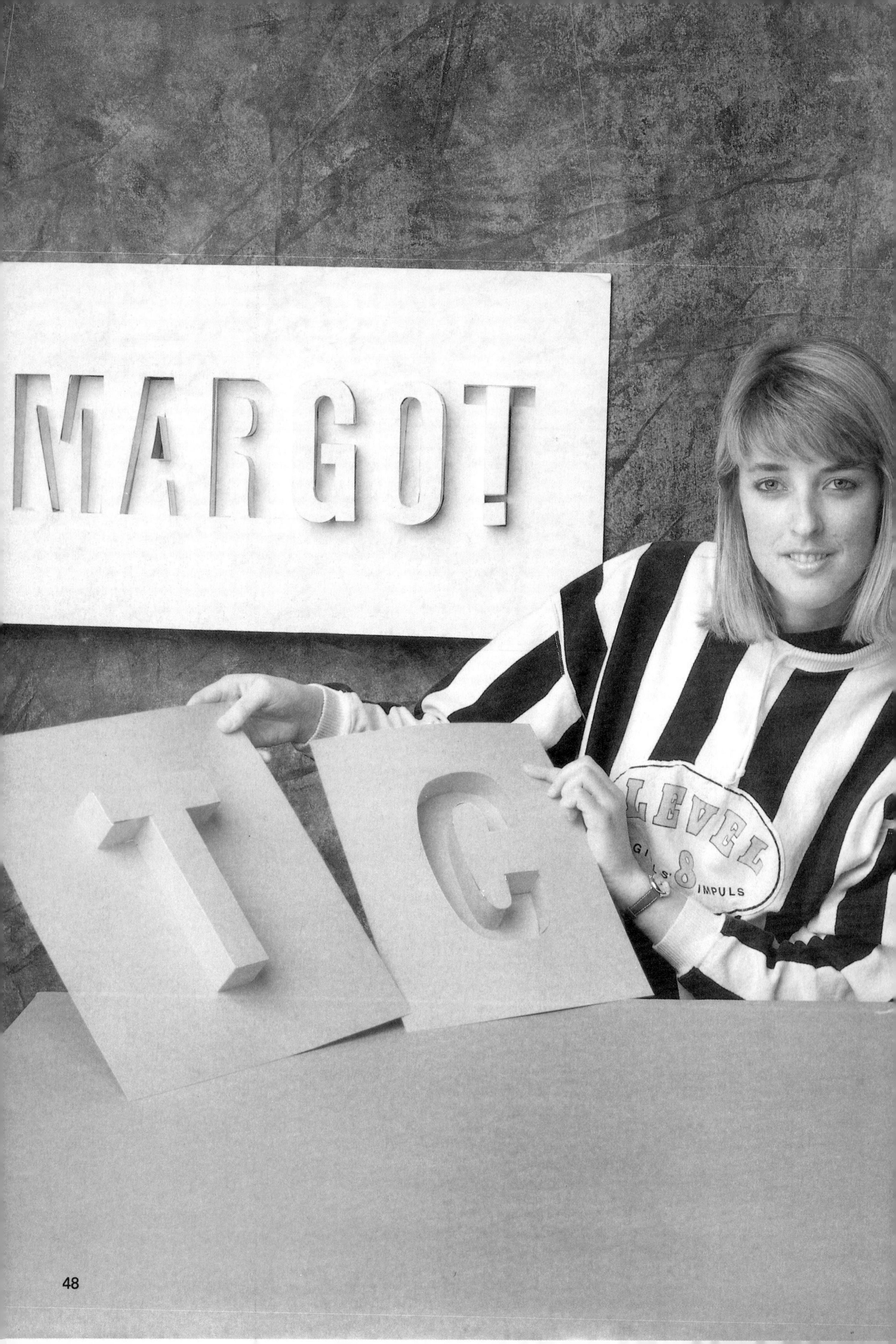
MARGOT!
T
C
LEVEL 8
GIRLS' IMPULS

JOANNA KIRK
MONSTER MASK

1 This is a messy and exciting way to create your own monster! Paint over a cardboard box (first making sure it'll go over your head comfortably). The box is your new head, so now for the features!

YOU WILL NEED

Cardboard box
Ready-mix paint
Cotton wool balls
Foil
Tissue paper

Bubble wrap
(packaging)
Glue
Sticky fixers

49

2 Joanna's monster has long flowing hair; stick long strips of bubble wrap (found in packaging) onto the top of the box.

3 Paint the strips of bubble wrap green; your monster can have any colour hair. Tear off strips of green tissue, scrumple up and stick onto the top of the box; this makes the 'hair' look curly.

4 When the hair is finished, create the monster face! Paint the giant eyes, mouth and teeth. Joanna's monster looks very hungry! The open mouth with jagged teeth help create that monster-look!

5 The finishing touch is a special pair of horns. Strips of kitchen foil are screwed up and stuck onto the box top using sticky tabs.

6 With a few more dabs and flicks of paint the monster is finished. Don't forget to make holes in the 'eyes' for you to look through. Allow the box to dry before trying it on. Give it a name and think what kind of voice your monster has.

7 As well as the head, using the same materials and larger cardboard boxes, you can make a monster body. Now all you have to wait for is a fancy dress party or Halloween!

Leila Jackson (14)

Sally White (12)

HAPPY JACK

Heidi Jane Noble (7)

Elizabeth & Helen Marsh (11 & 7)

GARDENS

A GARDEN IN A DISH

YOU WILL NEED

Old dish	paper (cellophane)
Sand	Silver foil
Stones	Moss, twigs, leaves
Transparent shiny blue	Green ink

1 To make your own mini-garden, first carefully collect some materials from the countryside, park or common. There is often a lot of moss growing along the banks of streams and rivers. Obviously you must be careful not to walk on private land or trample down flowers and shrubs!

2 Fallen leaves and twigs are very useful materials to use, but as Tony wants to create a mini-forest, he has taken a cutting from his fir tree.

3 Together with the stones and pebbles, all the materials have now been collected. Before he starts work Tony wants to colour the yellow sand green to make it look like grass.

4 If you use builders' sand, wash and sieve it first to make it fine.
Pour green ink into a lid and mix in the sand. Use a piece of wood to stir the mixture. Stop pouring in the ink when the sand has soaked it up. Leave to dry in an airing cupboard overnight.

5 Lay the silver foil on the base of the dish or plate. The blue cellophane is placed on top of the foil surface. Sprinkle the green sand, using a brush to push it into the best shape. Add the stones, pebbles and finally use the moss and fir twigs to create the 'forest'.

PALM HOUSE

YOU WILL NEED

Sheets of thin white
card

Plants

Thick green card
Double-sided tape
Scissors

1 Start with the base card; cut it out from a cardboard box, or make two
strips of green card and glue them together.
   Now cut out the five supporting strips and stick them onto the sides of the
base. The centre strip is the tallest (460mm × 250mm), the outside strips the
next tallest (350mm × 250mm), and the middle strips the lowest (270mm ×
250mm). These strips
need to be made of
stiff card.

2 Use thin white card to make the three arches
Carefully cut out strips within the card, no
forgetting to leave a flap at each end to stick th
strips to the supports. The card is 510mm long
220mm wide with 20mm gap
between the strips. Use double
sided tape or glue to stick the firs
arch over the central support an
onto the middle supports

3 Stick the side arch to the middle support and onto the base card. Repeat the same process with the last arch.

4 Now your palm house is ready, all you need are some palms! You could make your own plants out of tissue paper and foil. But using real plants is good because the leaves will grow through the strips.

GALLERY

Sarah Atkinson (6)

Rachael Wheatcroft (14)

Amanda Bearne (12)

HOLES

SILK SCREEN

YOU WILL NEED

Old picture frame or thick card	Paper
Net curtain	Scissors
Drawing pins	Double-sided
Thick paint	tape/adhesive

1 A silk screen press allows you to print through onto paper and material again and again. First you need to make a strong frame. Margot's frame is 340mm × 180mm, but it can be any size. Stick four side pieces together to make the frame. A thick old picture frame would do as well.

2 Lay the solid frame onto a sheet of net curtain. Stretch very tight and secure the curtain into the frame with pins.

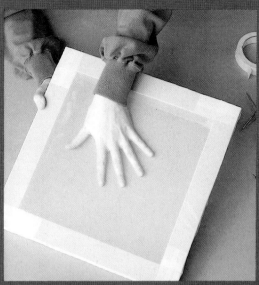

3 Make sure the curtain is as tight across the whole frame as possible.

4 Stick a stencil of the letter or pattern you want to print through onto the net curtain. Stick a base card to one side of the frame.

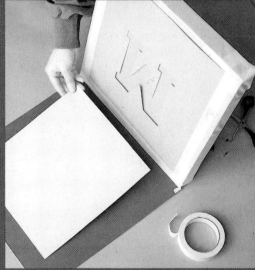

5 Now place the paper you want the print on between the stencil and the base card. The package is now complete. Next the paint!

6 Turn the frame over and pour a line of the thick paint along the top edge.

7 Using a thick piece of card mix in other colours and prepare to print.

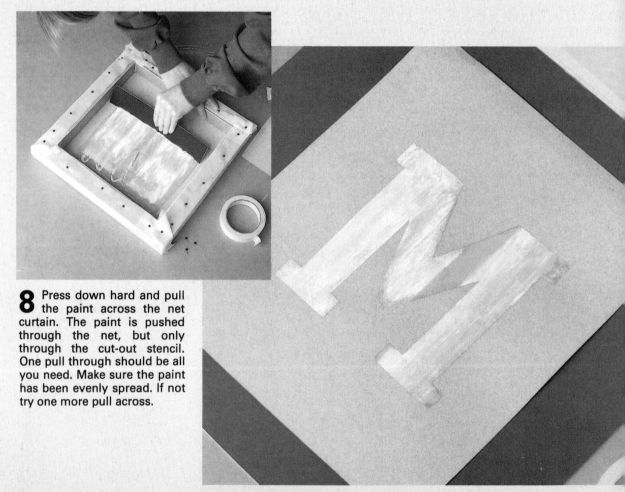

8 Press down hard and pull the paint across the net curtain. The paint is pushed through the net, but only through the cut-out stencil. One pull through should be all you need. Make sure the paint has been evenly spread. If not try one more pull across.

9 Lift up the frame to reveal the print. Using the same stencil you can add other colours and print as many letters, names or designs as you want.

You can use this press to print your name or design on T-shirts. Instead of paint, use colour fabric dyes, then it won't all disappear in the wash!

JOANNA KIRK
GROW YOUR OWN TREE

1 This is a big project which needs a bit of care. It's a quick way to grow your own tree without having to go into the garden!

4 Now to decorate your tree. Paper plates make ideal flowers! Cover them with foil. Cut and fold back the foil flaps to create the 'petals'.

2 Wearing old gloves to protect your hands, cut leaf shapes from a roll of chicken wire. Old scissors should be used, as the wire will ruin a new good pair! Bend the edges of the leaves inwards and leave a 'stem' at the end. This will allow you to attach them to the broom handle.

3 Cover a bucket with aluminium foil and secure a broom handle inside. Sand or rocks will keep it in position. Attach the leaves to the broom handle with wire.

5 Attach cotton wool balls or pot scourers to the centre of the plate for 'buds' and paint them different colours to complete the flower.

6 Using sticky tabs, secure the flowers to the leaves and stem.

7 When the tree is completed it will look great in any room!

TONY HART
PAPER CUTTING

YOU WILL NEED

Paper
Scissors
Cartridge paper
Cotton wool
Ink and water

1 Fold a square piece of paper into this triangle shape. Remember where the centre is and cut a triangle shape out of one of

2 Cut another triangle shape from the same side, turn the paper round and cut a lozenge-shape from the other side.

3 Unfold the paper to reveal an attractive geometric pattern. This is not the end! The pattern is now full of holes, so why not design a colourful background to complete the picture!

4 You can make all sorts of marvellous patterns by folding paper into a small size and cutting different shapes out of it.

5 Now soak a cotton wool ball in water and dampen the cartridge paper. While the paper is still wet drop ink or water colour paint onto the paper. The more colours you use the better. The wet colours will merge on their own, but if you tilt the paper you can direct the flow of these colours. Stunning effects can be created.

6 Allow the paper to dry and place the cut-out black paper on top. The colours can now be seen through the holes!

Kristel Haines (5)

Rebecca Smith (6)

Allison Goddard (11)

James Paddick (12)

COVERINGS

WRAPPING PAPER

YOU WILL NEED

(*There are three picture-making items in one here!*)

Paper to print on
Poster colour paints

Polystyrene shapes
Sponge
Textured wallpaper
Wax crayons/candle wax
Ink

2 Soak up some of the paint onto a sponge and dab the sponge over the polystyrene shape. Now print away! When the print gets a bit faded, dab more paint onto the polystyrene.

3 The good thing about using polystyrene is the textured pattern it makes. Continue printing until you've covered the paper.

1 Here are three quick ways to make your own wrapping paper designs. *a) Prints* · Mix up some red poster paint in a small tray. Carefully cut a triangle shape out of some polystyrene packaging. (It's best to use a craft knife.)

4 *b) Blobs* · Dampen the paper with a cotton wool ball soaked in clean water.

5 When the paper is still wet, drop coloured inks onto the surface and allow the colours to mix.

6 Tilting the paper will make the colours merge into each other, creating wonderful patterns.

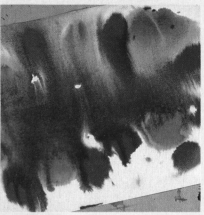

7 *c) Rubbings* · Place flimsy paper over a textured surface (old wallpaper, wood grain, even stone can be a good surface). Rub candle wax over the paper. You'll see nothing, but it is vital!

8 Soak ink into some cotton wool and spread the ink evenly over the surface of the paper. As if by magic, the textured surface pattern will suddenly

9 This pattern comes from old textured wallpaper. So by using *Prints, Blobs* and *Rubbings*, you can make endless sheets of colourful wrapping paper.

Matthew Miles Mclean (11)

Cara Inglesant (13)

Lucy Wight (7)

Catherine Cross (12)

HOMES & HOUSES

SCRATCH PICTURES

YOU WILL NEED

Card
Black India ink
Oil pastel/wax crayon
Black poster paint
Paintbrush

Sharp tool to scrape
with (broken pencil,
piece of sharp wood)

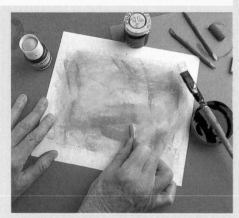

3 When the paint is dry, use a sharp piece of wood and scratch into the paint. As you scratch away you will reveal the wax coloured design beneath. Experiment with the type of scraping to produce the best results.

2 Paint over the design with a mixture of black poster paint and India ink. (This mixture will make sure the black paint does not crack when dry.)

1 To make this home-made scraper board, first cover white card with a wax crayon or oil pastel design. Make the colours thick and vivid!

TONY HART
MOSAIC COLLAGE

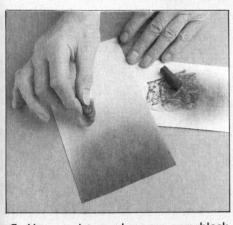

YOU WILL NEED

Black chalk
White card
Cotton wool

1 You need to make your own black dust for this item! Rub a piece of black chalk hard onto some card: this will create the right kind of dust. Using dry cotton wool, spread the black dust over white card. Start by rubbing hard to make the top of the card the blackest and gently grade the colour down the card leaving some white at the bottom.

2 Cut the card into thin strips and then into small squares. These squares do not need to be even; mosaics are made up of all sorts of different sizes.

3 Create your design by sticking the small squares onto a background card. Tony has graded his large card from black, dark grey to white using chalk dust.

Assemble your design by mixing up the tones of black, grey and white squares.

YOU WILL NEED

Postcard
Tracing paper
Ruler and pencil
Rubber
Large sheet of paper

Water-based paints
Paintbrushes

2 On trácing paper, carefully rule out a grid into 10mm squares. Trace off the design you want to enlarge.

3 Number the squares across and up the tracing paper. Now get a large sheet of paper and divide it into the same number of equal squares, but on a larger scale. Number the squares in the same way.

4 You can now copy the bus by checking and drawing its position in the square numbers on the large card. Rub out the grid lines and paint the big bus!

1 Here is a way of enlarging a picture. Joanna wants to paint a huge and accurate picture of this London bus. Using a small postcard, you first have to make a grid.

5 Using exactly the same technique you can grid up huge sheets of paper. In this way Joanna knows where to start her giant bus! Having drawn round the outline, by carefully trailing the paint, Joanna can now fill up the bus. Sponge dabs make the clouds look real, but it needs careful brush strokes to finish off the fine detail.

GALLERY

Christopher Lewry (5½)

Vicky Kington (7)

Darren Thomas (5)